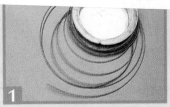

1

Tigertail is easy to use and recommended for heavy glass, ceramic and stone beads.

Tigertail is actually fine wire strands twisted together and coated with nylon. It comes in different colors and weights; use heavier wire with heavier beads. The .012 weight is strong enough to support even heavy beads, yet narrow enough to be doubled back through most beads.

2

Because tigertail is too stiff to knot, always secure it with a crimp bead (see page 9). If a chain is desired which is too thick to go through the beads, cut it where you want the beads to hang and attach a length of tigertail with a crimp bead. After stringing the beads, crimp the other end to the next piece of chain.

3

Push the middle of a short chain length through the hole in a large bead, then pull the ends around and through the loop in the chain. Now simply thread the tigertail through the end links and you have a dangling focus bead. Here, a brass disk bead is added around the doubled chain.

3

beading needle

1

NYLON BEADING THREAD

Nylon thread is used with a twisted-wire beading needle to string light-weight beads such as seed beads. The needle makes it easier to thread than monofilament. First attach one thread end to a clasp (see #3 below), then pull the other end through the needle and flatten the eye around it.

2

Beading thread is commonly used with pearls and semi-precious beads, knotting between them for security. Slide a bead into place and make an overhand knot in the thread. Before tightening it, insert a needle through the knot. While pulling the thread, slide the knot close against the bead.

3

There are several ways to finish a necklace strung on thread. One simple method is to tie each end to a clasp, then thread the tail back through the first few beads and trim the excess.

Several strands can be joined in an end cap (see page 13), or each end secured with a bead tip (see page 4).

A tiny knot between each pair of pearls allows the strand to move with the flowing grace that suits them and keeps the pearls from scraping against each other. If the strand ever breaks, the knots will prevent all but one or two pearls from falling to the ground.

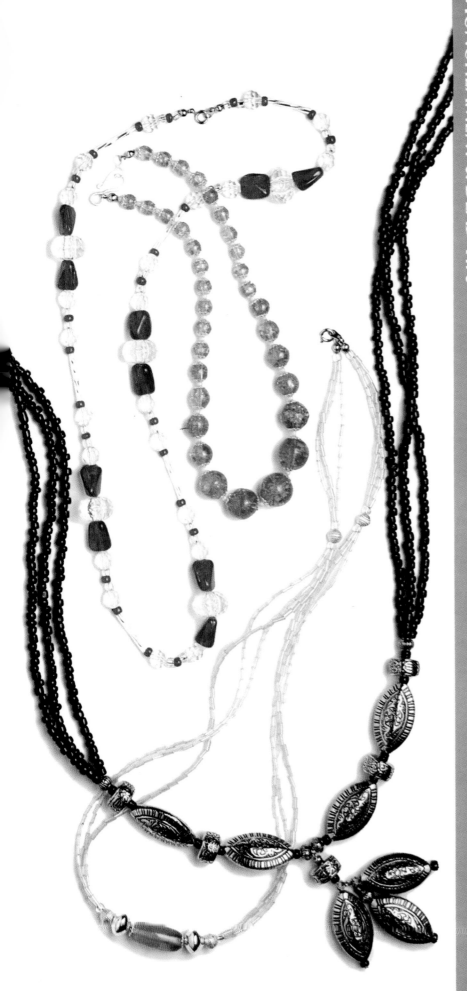

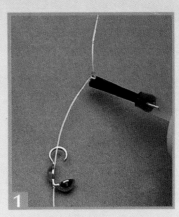

4

1 String small and medium-sized beads on nylon monofilament, which resembles fishing line. It is very strong and comes in several weights. Because it is nearly invisible, it's especially effective when used with clear beads. Coat monofilament knots with clear nail polish to secure them.

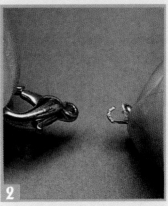

2 I recommend bead tips for attaching monofilament to a clasp. Thread the end through the hole in the tip and knot two or three times so it can't slip back through. Attach the tip to the clasp. Because the knot is visible in this open-style bead tip, use it for simple, single-strand necklaces.

3 A double-sided bead tip is also available. It closes like a clam shell over a knot and looks like a small metal bead. For a dangle, close one over the head of a head pin. Bead the head pin (see page 11) and loop the end. Insert a jump ring through the loop and hang other beaded head pins from it.

5

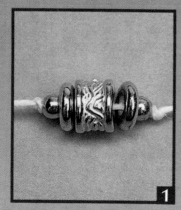

Many different cording materials are available for beading: waxed linen or nylon, suede and round leather, satin or rattail, and elastic. All come in varying weights—be sure your cord fits through your beads. For added interest and texture (with fewer beads!) knot the cord to leave empty lengths between beads.

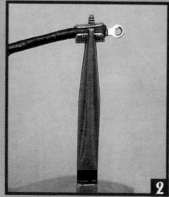

Cording crimps are the easiest way to secure cording ends to a clasp. Apply E-6000™ or Goop™ glue to the end, then place it in the small tray of the crimp. While holding it in place, use pliers to press the sides over the cord securely. Use jump rings to attach the loops of the crimp to the clasp.

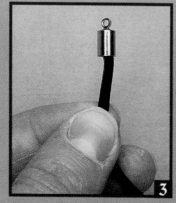

A cord cap is a cylinder with a loop on one end. Apply glue to the cord end and insert it into the cap—be sure to use glue or cement which adheres to metal. Allow to dry before handling. Crimps or caps and glue will prevent fraying of satin cording.

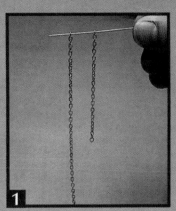

1

Often a length of chain between necklace elements adds sparkle and sophistication to an otherwise plain piece. To cut even chain lengths without counting links, cut one the desired length. Slip the end link on a pin, then slip an end of the remaining chain beside it. Cut to match; repeat.

2

For the black and gold necklace, equal lengths of chain connect beaded eye pins (see page 12). Open the eye, insert it through an end link and close it again. Repeat to finish the necklace.

3

If the holes in the beads are large enough, they can be strung directly onto the chain as in the silver necklace. (See page 2, #3, for another method of using chain to attach a focal bead.) Attach a clasp to a chain by inserting a jump ring through the end link and the clasp loop.

6

1

Some of the clasps available for necklaces are: barrel (A), insertion-type closures (B, C) hook and eye (D, E), spring ring (F) and lobster claw (G). Multiple strands can be attached to a regular single-strand clasp or to one with several loops.

2

To use a multiple-strand clasp, attach one end of a strand to a loop on one side of the clasp. Bead or finish the strand as desired, then attach the other end to the corresponding loop on the other side. It is easiest to get the strands in the correct loops if the clasp remains closed as you work.

back view

3

Another use for a lobster claw clasp is to attach it to a pendant so the piece can be removed and hung on another beaded necklace or chain to create a new look. A wrist watch makes an unusual pendant; gold tube beads were added on each side to keep the clasp centered and hide the bars.

Hang a watch with the top down so that the wearer can lift it up to read it.

right

wrong

Jump rings are available in varying sizes and colors of metal. They are used to link jewelry elements as shown above. They can be added to lengthen and loosen a necklace or bracelet. To open a jump ring, grasp each side with a pair of pliers. Push one side, holding the other still. Do not pull the ends apart; this weakens the ring.

Choose a jump ring large enough to fit through all the elements being linked. For the dangles on this red and gray necklace, I placed three seed beads on each of fourteen 8mm silver jump rings and was still able to insert them, in pairs, through the loops of beaded eye pins (see page 12).

split ring

Looking like miniature key rings, split rings are used when jump rings are not strong enough. They will not pull open, even under the weight of heavy beads, so I use them as loops for many clasps. A large split ring can be the focus of a necklace, with dangles attached as shown here.

9

crimp
bead

These soft metal beads, also called "French crimps," are most often used to secure tigertail or other strands to clasps. Thread a strand through the crimp bead, then through a loop of the clasp. Double the end back into the bead and pull through 1". Slide the bead close to the clasp.

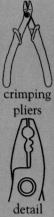

crimping
pliers

detail

Squeeze the bead tightly in the wide hole of crimping pliers. This will flatten it around both tigertail strands and indent one side. The flattened crimp bead keeps the wire from sliding free.

Insert the bead into the round hole of the pliers with the fold toward the jaws. Squeeze to fold it over onto itself, making it round. After beading the strand, add another crimp and the other half of the clasp. Double the wire back through the crimp and the first few beads; pull snugly to remove slack. Squeeze the crimp and trim the excess wire.

The center area of a necklace can include additional strands with the help of crimp beads. The blue and silver necklace shown here is an example of a single strand with multiple strands through the center.

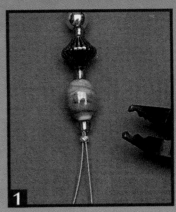

For a single-to-multiple strand necklace, crimp a tigertail strand to a clasp. Then bead a third of the length and add a crimp. Slip one or more additional strands through the crimp and the last few beads; squeeze the crimp. Bead each strand separately, adding more beads to the strands which you want to be longer.

Slide another crimp over all the strands and secure it close to the last beads. Trim all the strands but one to $1/2$" and bead that strand in a mirror image of the first third of the necklace, sliding the first few beads down to cover all the wire ends.

Another use for crimp beads is to secure beads onto stick pins and earring wires. Since these pins and wires are heavier than the beading strands, it takes a little extra strength to secure the crimps.

11

head pin

1

Dangles are most easily made on head pins. Looking like blunt straight pins, these are available in different colors and lengths. After beading a head pin, use wire cutters to trim the end to ³⁄₈"–¹⁄₂" for finishing.

looping a head pin

2

Use round-nose pliers to bend the head pin just above the last bead, then to round the end into a loop. The loop can be threaded on a neck-lace or inserted through a loop on an earring finding or medallion. For a looser dangle, hang it on a jump ring.

3

The "bib" on the gold and silver necklace is made of seven head pins of graduated lengths, each beaded in a slightly more complex pattern. Because they are threaded directly onto the strand, they hang more rigidly than the blue glass dangles, which are attached with jump rings.

Head pins are also available with round heads for the rich look of an additional tiny bead.

The loops of the eye pins attach the pieces of these stacked dangles.

12

eye pin

The loop on the end of this blunt pin is called its "eye." Like head pins, eye pins are available in various sizes and colors. Bead an eye pin, then trim and loop its end (see page 11, #2). With a loop on each end, a beaded eye pin links jewelry elements.

For a jointed necklace or bracelet, link beaded eye pins together. Carefully open one loop and insert a loop of the next pin, then close it. Repeat for the desired length. The shimmer of the metal loops gives a delicate sparkle and the look of chain.

Eye pins can be beaded like head pins for dangles, the difference being the exposed loop on the bottom. "Stacked dangles" can be made by hanging another eye pin, head pin, drop bead or locket from the loop. For these earrings, three seed beads are placed on each eye before beading the pin.

1

The beads at the strand ends must be small enough for all of them to fit inside the end cap.

A multiple strand necklace usually needs an end cap to pull the strands together and hide knots or crimps. Knot or crimp the strand ends together and trim the excess thread or tiger-tail. Open an eye pin (see page 12) and insert it between the strands, then close the eye around them.

2

Insert the straight end of the eye pin through the hole of the end cap, pulling the strand ends up into the cap. Trim and loop the pin (see page 11, #2). Hook the loop into the clasp and close it.

3

For a multi-strand necklace with single-strand sides, bead the side strands and crimp each to a jump ring. Bead the center strands, finish with end caps and attach one end to each jump ring. (See page 10, #1, for another technique.)

The fuchsia and silver necklace uses only one cap on each glass bead.

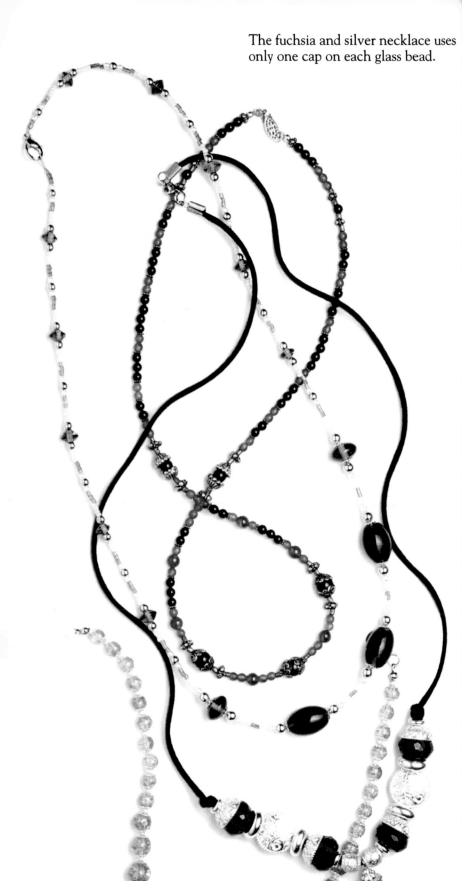

The blue glass necklace has a cap on each side of each bead, with seed beads between as separators.

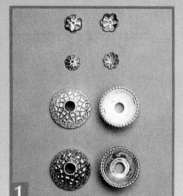

Bead caps add sparkle and make plain beads look extra special. A bead cap is cup-shaped with a hole in the center. The cup fits around the side of a bead and the caps can be used on both sides or just on one side of a bead. Make sure the cap fits over the bead when purchasing it.

To add bead caps to certain beads, thread the first cap onto the strand, then the bead, then the second cap. Make sure the caps are threaded to "cup" around the bead.

Bead caps can also highlight center drop or dangle beads, adding importance to them. Thread the bead on a head or eye pin (see pages 11–12), then the cap, cup side down. Add any other beads and caps, then finish the dangle.

Use spacer bars to shape a bracelet or collar necklace to lie flat. They separate multiple strands, preventing the tangling which would weaken the strands. Bead all the strands at once, adding an extra seed bead or two if needed to even the strands.

The bar on each side of a watch face is a perfect anchor for the tigertail strands (see page 1). On the turquoise watch, the bars were removed and two large-holed beads were placed on each to cover them.

Fold-over watch clasps are very secure and are available with holes for three strands. Close the clasp while attaching the strands to make sure they are correctly placed and the band is not twisted.

The coiled bracelet is beaded on 'memory wire." To secure the beads, loop the end with roundnose pliers.

This bracelet is clasped by passing a bead at one end (see #1 at right) through a loop at the other.

The silver toggle clasp, with its ring and bar design, reflects the forms of the silver disk beads and the blue ring bead.

Several options are available when finishing bracelets. This clasp, made especially for bracelets, is curved to fit comfortably over the wrist.

This bracelet is strung on waxed linen. See #3 at the right for instructions on its sliding clasp.

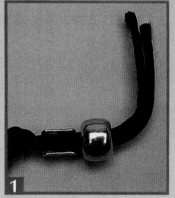

1

For the black and silver bracelet, fold black satin cording in half and knot ½" from the fold to make a loop. Hold the ends together to bead and knot as shown at left. After the last knot, add a cording crimp which has the loop cut off, then one more bead. Fold the ends back into the crimp and secure; trim the ends.

2

The gold medallion was made by gluing a bead on a pendant finding. Push the center of 10" of black waxed linen through a hole in the edge and pull the ends around through the loop. Bead the ends, separately where a double strand is desired and together otherwise, and knot, leaving 2" tails.

3

Insert the tails of one side through two beads and knot the very end so they won't slip off. Repeat with the other tails, inserting them through the same two beads but in the opposite direction. The two beads slide to enlarge the bracelet to fit over the hand, then slide back for a snug fit.

Use E-6000™ or Goop™ Arts & Crafts® glue to attach the pad of a post to the back of a bead. Posts are available in various metals, including hypoallergenic sterling, stainless and gold-plated. Pads come in sizes, and flat or cupped, to fit different beads.

Dangles made from head or eye pins (see pages 11, 12) can be hung from many different findings. Fishhook earwires and some styles of post earrings come with loops at the bottom to attach dangles. To assure that multiple dangles hang side-by-side nicely, use a jump ring to attach each one.

Fingernail clasps with posts are a less common earring finding. More secure than fishhooks but without a back to get lost, they have a distinctive style with a hint of glamour. Bead a large jump ring (these are 15mm with stacked dangles) and slip it over the back of the clasp.

To bead the fishhook head pin or large kidney wire earrings, straighten them for beading, then bend back into shape.